BOOK ANALYSIS

By Anna Savory

A Christmas Carol

BY CHARLES DICKENS

CHARLES DICKENS

ENGLISH NOVELIST AND SOCIAL CRITIC

- **Born in Portsmouth in 1812.**
- **Died in Higham in 1870.**
- **Notable works:**
  - *Oliver Twist* (1837), novel
  - *Great Expectations* (1860), novel
  - *A Tale of Two Cities* (1859), novel

Charles Dickens was born in Portsmouth in 1812, the second of eight children, and spent his early childhood moving back and forth between London and Kent. He was a bookish child with a great deal of academic promise, but when his father was sent to the infamous Marshalsea debtor's prison in 1824, Dickens was forced to leave school and take up a position in a blacking (shoe polish) factory, a situation which fostered in him a life-long passion for the rights of the working classes and of working-class children in particular. Despite his lack of formal education, he secured work as a legal clerk and later as a political journalist. His journalistic pieces were collected and published in 1836 under the title *Sketches By Boz* (Boz being his nom de plume and family nickname), and his first serialised novel *The Pickwick Papers* (1836-1837) followed shortly afterwards. *The Pickwick Papers* was a critical and popular hit and signalled the beginning of a period of immense productivity and literary success. Over the coming years Dickens (while also maintaining editorships and journalistic positions) would pen numerous novels in quick succession, including *Oliver Twist* (1837-1839), *Nicholas Nickleby* (1838-1839), *The Old Curiosity Shop* (1840-1841) and *Barnaby Rudge* (1841). His novels, despite their clear socio-political agenda, were met with almost universal praise, transforming him into an international literary celebrity, popular both with the upper classes (he counted Queen Victoria [English monarch, 1819-1901] among his fans) and the illiterate working classes (who would attend monthly public readings of his work). Enjoyed in equal measure for his humour and larger than life characters as well as for his blistering social commentaries, Dickens' reputation as a literary colossus and writer addressing and embodying the concerns of the period was well-established even during his lifetime and, indeed, persists today, with the term 'Dickensian' having become synonymous with any and all things mid-Victorian.

A CHRISTMAS CAROL

DICKENS' FESTIVE MORAL LESSON

- **Genre:** novella
- **Reference edition:** Dickens, C. (2003) *A Christmas Carol and Other Christmas Writings*. London: Penguin.
- **1st edition:** 1843
- **Themes:** poverty, social injustice, miserliness vs generosity, redemption, Christmas spirit, family, social responsibility

A novella divided into five chapters (or 'staves', as Dickens termed them), *A Christmas Carol* tells the story of Ebenezer Scrooge, an elderly money-lender and miser who despises Christmas and the generosity of spirit that accompanies it. He is ultimately transformed and redeemed when he is visited on Christmas Eve, first by the tortured ghost of his former business partner Jacob Marley and then by three spirits: the Ghosts of Christmas Past, Present and Future.

Optimistic, festive and heart-warming, *A Christmas Carol* was written at a time when Victorian society was starting to re-examine both itself and its Christmas traditions (attributing new meaning and social significance to them accordingly), and is an argument for a new, more generous and embracive social outlook (which Dickens would go on to term his 'Carol Philosophy') as much as it is a critique of existing social injustice. Phenomenally popular with critics and the general public alike, *A Christmas Carol* was published on 17 December 1843 and had sold over 5000 copies by Christmas Eve. It has not been out of print since.

SUMMARY

MARLEY'S GHOST

Ebenezer Scrooge is the sole owner of his money-lending business following the death of his business partner Jacob Marley seven years earlier. We are introduced to him in his counting-house on a bleak Christmas Eve. He expresses his intense dislike for Christmas (and mercantile world-view) by rejecting his nephew's invitation to Christmas dinner with the reminder that Christmas is a time "for paying bills without money; [and ...] finding yourself a year older, but not an hour richer" (p. 36). He also turns away two men seeking charitable donations (telling them that there are workhouses and prisons for the poor, and that if they cannot use them then they ought to die in order to "reduce the surplus population", p. 39) and slams the door in the face of a young carol singer. He grudgingly allows his clerk, Bob Cratchit, to take Christmas Day off, but tells him to "be here all the earlier the next morning" (p. 41).

That night, on returning to his lodgings, Scrooge witnesses his door knocker transform into the face of his former business partner Jacob Marley. He brushes it off as a trick of the mind but is startled when a disused bell which still hangs in his rooms begins to ring of its own accord. The ringing is followed by the sound of chains dragging across the floor and Marley's ghost bursts from the cellar, shackled by "cash-boxes, keys, padlocks, ledgers, deeds and heavy purses wrought in steel" (p. 44). Terrified. Scrooge attempts to deny the ghost's existence, but is disturbed by its "death-cold eyes" (*ibid.*) as well as the infernal implications of the way its hair, skirts and tassels move as if "agitated by the hot vapour from an oven" (p. 47). Marley's ghost explains that it is condemned to walk the earth experiencing the "incessant torture of remorse" (p. 48) and bound in the chains it "forged in life" from its own greed and selfishness (p. 47). Marley warns that the same fate awaits Scrooge (and that his chain is even longer) but that he has procured his old friend "a chance and hope of escaping [his] fate" (p. 50). Scrooge is overjoyed until the ghost explains that in order to win his redemption Scrooge will be haunted by three further ghosts, who will appear to him that night.

Marley then "floats out upon the bleak, dark night" to join a cloud of similarly tortured "phantoms" (p. 52), many of whom Scrooge recognises from life. Scrooge tries to brush off the events with a trademark "humbug!" but cannot get past the first syllable.

THE FIRST OF THE THREE SPIRITS

As Marley's ghost predicted, the first spirit visits Scrooge as the clock strikes one. It announces itself as "The Ghost of Christmas Past" (p. 55), and leads Scrooge through the wall of his bedroom and out onto a country lane which he recognises from his childhood. The spirit explains that the world they now inhabit is "but [a] shadow [...] of the things that have been" (p. 57), that they cannot be observed and that the figures they will be observing have no consciousness. Scrooge leads them by memory to his old school and they watch a young Scrooge, who is staying there alone over the Christmas break with only books and his own imagination for company. Scrooge weeps for his lonely childhood and explains to the spirit that there was "a boy singing A Christmas Carol at [his] door last night [and he] should like to have given him something" (p. 59).

The spirit declares that they will see "another Christmas" (*ibid.*) and they watch as young Scrooge, and the classroom he sits in, age a few years. Young Scrooge's little sister Fan enters and announces to her brother that he is to come home for Christmas this year as their father is "so much kinder than he used to be" (p. 60).

The spirit transports them both forward in time to a Christmas party thrown by Scrooge's former employer Mr Fezziwig, a jovial, exuberant boss who delights in hosting extravagant Christmas balls for his employees. Scrooge, moved by how happy and grateful the attendees of the ball are, remarks to the spirit that he should like to speak to his clerk Bob Cratchit. The ballroom dissolves and they view another vision together. Scrooge watches himself, now "a man in the prime of life" with a face "beginning to wear the signs of care and avarice" (p. 65). A young woman, Belle, with whom he was once romantically involved, explains to him that his love for her is being replaced by his love of money and that she can no longer be with him. Scrooge begs the spirit to take him home, but it shows him one last scene. They watch Belle, years later, with a large and boisterous family including a beautiful young daughter. Her husband returns with Christmas gifts for all, and sits, in calm domestic bliss with his wife and daughter by the fireplace, remarking to Belle that he "saw an old friend of hers [...] Mr Scrooge" that afternoon, and that he was "quite alone in the world." (p. 68). Scrooge demands that the spirit take him home, and attempts to extinguish its crown of light with its own extinguisher cap. He succeeds, and finding himself in his room again, falls asleep, exhausted.

THE SECOND OF THE THREE SPIRITS

Scrooge wakes again at the (second) stroke of one but is surprised to find no spirit at his bedside. At length he follows a beam of light to an adjoining room and meets the Ghost of Christmas Present, a jovial giant, clothed in green velvet and enthroned on a pile of seasonal food. The two of them visit a joyous Christmas market and watch local people preparing for, and celebrating Christmas Day. They visit the home of Scrooge's clerk, Bob Cratchit, and we are introduced to his poor but happy family including his youngest son Tiny Tim, who is severely crippled. Scrooge asks the spirit if Tiny Tim will live and it replies that it "see[s] a vacant seat" at the table the following year "if these shadows remain unaltered by the Future" (p. 82). Scrooge is upset by the news and overcome with guilt when the spirit reminds him of his earlier comments on how death would "reduce the surplus population" (*ibid*.). The Cratchits drink a bitter toast to Scrooge's health, and he realises that he is "the ogre of the family" and the man directly responsible for their poverty (p. 83).

Scrooge and the spirit visit the Christmas gatherings of a miner family and of a group of lighthouse workers, both of whom, though poor, have an abundance of Christmas spirit. They also view Scrooge's nephew's Christmas Day. Full of laughter and good cheer, Scrooge's nephew and his wife discuss Scrooge, and while most of the party find him either laughable, hateful, or both, his nephew admits to feeling "sorry for him" and explains that the only real victim of Scrooge's behaviour is Scrooge himself (p. 87).

Scrooge and the spirit stay for the entire evening, watching the Christmas party which Scrooge could have been part of had he accepted his nephew's invitation. Scrooge joins in with the parlour games in spite of both himself and the fact that his answers cannot be heard by anyone other than the spirit. Eventually they leave the party and the Ghost of Christmas Present reveals two emaciated children who have been hidden beneath his cloak throughout. He explains to Scrooge that they are Ignorance and Want and that he should beware them both. Scrooge asks whether there is "no refuge or resource" (p. 94) that could help the children, and the spirit repeats back to him his earlier comments on the poorhouses mockingly before vanishing. Scrooge looks about for him and sees instead "a solemn Phantom" floating like mist towards him (*ibid.*).

THE LAST OF THE SPIRITS

The Phantom approaches Scrooge, and when it stands "tall and stately beside him" he is filled with "uncertain horror" (p. 95). He asks if it is "The Ghost of Christmas Yet to Come" and it does not answer but points "onward with its hand" (*ibid.*).

Scrooge follows the Phantom into the future and to the City of London, where he listens as a group of businessmen discuss the death of an unnamed man. They observe that the funeral is likely to be "very cheap" (p. 97) and poorly attended but agree to go on the condition that there is free lunch. Scrooge looks to the spirit for an explanation and it shows him two important, powerful men whom Scrooge has always admired. They acknowledge the death of the same man briefly, stating that "Old Scratch [the devil] has got his own at last" before moving on to discuss the weather instead (*ibid.*). Confused as to why he is witnessing such trivial conversations, Scrooge looks about for his future self in the crowds before being led by the spirit into a poor and disreputable area. They witness an exchange at a pawn shop where a laundress, maid and undertaker's assistant attempt to sell a dead man's stolen belongings. They admit that their behaviour is mercenary but agree that "every person has a right to take care of themselves. [As] *he* always did" (p. 99).

Scrooge realises that there is a parallel between "this unhappy man" (p. 102) and himself, and is appalled when the spirit shows him the man's body, laid out on his ransacked deathbed, completely alone. He asks the spirit if there is a single person who "feels emotion caused by this man's death" (p. 103) and is transported to the house of a young couple who owed the dead man money and are now freed from their debt. When Scrooge specifies that he meant "tenderness connected with a death" (p. 104) rather than delight, the spirit takes him to the Cratchits' house once more.

The Cratchits do not discuss the death of the unnamed man, but are collectively mourning the now deceased Tiny Tim who is greatly missed. They resolve to honour his memory by being more patient and loving towards each other than ever. Scrooge senses that the vision is almost over and asks the spirit who the dead man is. The spirit leads him to a churchyard and directs him with an "inexorable finger" to his own grave (p. 107). Scrooge drops to the floor and repents, promising "to honour Christmas in [his] heart, and [...] keep it all the year" if it will "sponge away the writing on [the] stone" (p. 110). As he grasps imploringly at the spirit's cloak it shrinks and collapses, eventually taking on the form of his own bedpost.

THE END OF IT

Scrooge wakes in his own rooms a transformed and redeemed man. He throws open his window and calls to a boy in the street, asking him what day it is. The boy replies that it is Christmas Day and Scrooge, happy that he has not missed it, and that the visions all took place in a single night, asks the boy to go to the butcher's and buy the largest turkey they have. He offers him a shilling for the errand and half a crown if he does it quickly. He sends the turkey to the Cratchits' house (paying for a hansom cab to transport it) and walks about the streets of London enjoying the Christmas scenes. On the way he meets one of the men who asked him for a charitable donation the day before and gives him an unspecified but incredibly large sum of money. In the afternoon he visits his nephew and experiences first-hand the wonderful party he observed with the Ghost of Christmas Present. He surprises Bob Cratchit at work the following day, at first feigning his old, cruel manner before revealing that he is a new man and promising to help relieve the Cratchits' poverty by being a kinder, more generous employer. Dickens notes that Scrooge was "better than his word" (p. 116), that Tiny Tim did not die, and that from that point on Scrooge "knew how to keep Christmas well" (p. 119). He closes with an appeal to his readers that the same might "be truly said of [...] all of us" (*ibid.*).

CHARACTER STUDY

EBENEZER SCROOGE

An elderly miser, Ebenezer Scrooge runs a London counting house (a Victorian term for an accountancy firm/money-lending business). "A tight-fisted hand at the grindstone" (p. 34), Scrooge is a covetous, cruel misanthrope, who projects an emotional (and at times, Dickens implies, a physical) coldness. He despises Christmas and the generosity of spirit it inspires in others, dismissing both as "humbug" (p. 35). By the end of the novella he has undergone a complete transformation of character, becoming a generous, sociable, public-spirited man who promises to "honour Christmas in [his] heart and keep it all the year" (p. 110), and he wins his redemption accordingly.

JACOB MARLEY

Jacob Marley was Scrooge's former business partner and the only person who could match Scrooge for miserliness and cruelty. He dies seven years before the novella begins (as mentioned in its famous opening line). Scrooge was his "sole mourner" (p. 33) and Dickens implies that even he was not particularly affected by Marley's death.

Marley's ghost visits Scrooge in the first stave, bound in chains made of "cash-boxes, keys, padlocks, ledgers, deeds, and heavy purses wrought in steel" (p. 44). He explains that he is condemned to wander the world of men, dragging behind him the chains he "forged in life" (p. 47) with his own acts of greed (and however much he may be able to move freely through the world, the fact that his clothes and hair move independently as if "agitated [...] by the hot vapour from an oven" (*ibid.*) make it clear that he is also in hell). He is responsible for putting in place a ghostly scheme to help his old friend avoid the same fate.

THE GHOST OF CHRISTMAS PAST

The Ghost of Christmas Past is the first spirit to visit Scrooge, and possesses the ability to transport him through time to view "shadows of what has been" (p. 57). It appears both old and young simultaneously, and has a constantly fluctuating physical form, but for the most part resembles a child in a white dress, holding a sprig of holly, and crowned with light (the intensity of which correlates with the strength of Scrooge's emotion). It has "a great extinguisher" (p. 55) (candle snuffer) under one arm with which Scrooge eventually extinguishes it (symbolising his forcible suppression of his own memories).

As with all the spirits, the Ghost of Christmas Past has an innate knowledge of Scrooge's motivations and behaviour, and it mildly (though still with a sense of irony) draws his attention to discrepancies between how he feels when watching the visions and how he behaves in daily life.

THE GHOST OF CHRISTMAS PRESENT

The second spirit to visit Scrooge, the Ghost of Christmas Present, is a huge bare-chested "jolly Giant" (p. 72) who, when we first meet him, is enthroned on a pile of Christmas food including "turkeys, geese, game [...] plum pudding [... and] immense twelfth cakes" (*ibid.*). His good cheer and excess deliberately recalls the medieval Baronial feasting that Victorian readers would have nostalgically associated with Christmas, and which was a key part of the Christmas revival of the 1840s. He accompanies Scrooge on a tour of his contemporaries' Christmases, including the Cratchits' Christmas and his nephew Fred's Christmas party. As with the Ghost of Christmas Past, the Ghost of Christmas Present has full knowledge of Scrooge's behaviour, though it is more mocking in its corrections, pointedly and ironically repeating Scrooge's own statements on charity and the poor back to him.

THE GHOST OF CHRISTMAS YET TO COME

The Ghost of Christmas Yet To Come is the third and final spirit that Scrooge meets. It is a hovering, cowled "Phantom" (p. 95) that cannot speak but only points ominously. Its appearance deliberately recalls Death (as an anthropomorphised figure), and indeed its entire vision centres on Scrooge's own death. While it cannot communicate verbally with Scrooge, it is sentient, and does respond to his requests, though in this it also shows some of the mocking spirit of its predecessors, as when Scrooge asks to see "any person" who feels "emotion" at his death (p. 103) (i.e. anyone who is grieving), the spirit conducts him to the home of a couple who are overjoyed.

BOB CRATCHIT

Scrooge's mild-mannered and dutiful clerk. Although he is extremely poor, with a large family to support, he is kind, generous, and cannot bring himself speak ill of his employer. He is a doting father and is particularly attached to his ailing son Tiny Tim, whom he carries to and from church on his shoulders.

TINY TIM

Bob Cratchit's son, Tiny Tim is upbeat and hopeful despite being severely crippled. Universally beloved by his family and community, he is sweet, kind, and devout, possessing a piousness beyond his years.

FRED

Fred is Scrooge's nephew and his only living relative. He is his polar opposite in every respect: an effusive, affable, witty young man with a "contagious" laugh (p. 87), who counters Scrooge's bitter comments on Christmas and humanity with good-natured ease, stating that Christmas "has done [him] good, and *will* do [him] good [...

and so] God bless it!" (p. 37). He has considerable insight into Scrooge's situation, pitying him and characterising him as "comical old fellow" (p. 87) rather than an evil man; he also ultimately recognises that the only person really being damaged by Scrooge's behaviour is Scrooge himself.

ANALYSIS

SELF VS SOCIETY: SCROOGE'S SECULAR AND SPIRITUAL REDEMPTION

Redemption is the thematic heart of *A Christmas Carol*, and Dickens made it clear that he intended the novella to function as a spiritual (or rather, sociological) sermon as much as a heart-warming story. Scrooge's experiences are presented as a moral lesson to the mid-Victorian audience, who were hemmed in by, but increasingly aware of, their unforgiving attitudes towards the poor, that redemption and transformation (even in the most unlikely cases) were not just possible but essential. Dickens, for all he asserts that he is standing "at [the reader's] elbow" (p. 54) is also very much in the pulpit. It is fitting therefore that his presentation of redemption plays into established religious narratives of redemptive suffering. Alongside this, however, there is a strong secular or sociological element; Scrooge's redemption hinges upon a reconsideration of self and community, and a series of social and personal revelations without which redemptive suffering simply would not occur. His redemption in the eyes of society and in relation to his own self is, to some extent, more important than his spiritual redemption for Dickens, although the two do go hand in hand.

For all that *A Christmas Carol* bills itself as a 'ghost story', it is perhaps more accurately an allegory, or rather a series of parables which build on each other successively. Dickens was clear that his intention was to set forth a moral code for his readers, a new 'Carol Philosophy' that everyone should aspire to, and indeed he closes the piece with an aside stating that he trusts all readers will apply Scrooge's lessons to their own life. The idea of Scrooge as a figure redeemed by suffering, in the traditional penitential sense, is therefore only in keeping with the moralising tone. We see Scrooge undergo a traditional pattern of suffering, repentance, and subsequent transformation; beginning the story as a "covetous old sinner" (p. 34) (note the religious terminology), and ending it "as good a man as the good old city knew" (p. 116). In the interim he is subject to what amounts to emotional torture and pointed humiliation, which eventually leaves him supplicant before his own grave "holding up his hands in a last prayer to have his fate reversed" (p. 110) (his 'fate' meaning both his terrestrial fate of dying a lonely, bitter death and his eternal fate, which is to say Marley's fate: damnation). The imagery feeds into an established Christian narrative on repentance and redemption via suffering that Dickens' mid-Victorian audience would certainly have been familiar with.

That said, Scrooge's redemptive process is also a secular and profoundly psychological one. His redemption is predicated on a change in his social values, and this change is, in and of itself, redemptive. The visions presented to him by the ghosts, though distressing, humiliating and traumatic, are not primarily intended as punishments; instead he is being made to understand why he should be punished, and that knowledge is a punishment in itself.

Scrooge's redemption therefore is not just achieved through straightforward suffering but rather a socio-psychological process, beginning with the tearing down of ego and ending with a complete reassessment of the self in relation to society. Dickens shows Scrooge's sense of selfhood dissolving and his sense of community growing in stages; a process which begins with his first ghostly visitation and increases with each spirit. Marley's ghost elicits a fear and vulnerability at odds with Scrooge's "hard, sharp" (p. 34) exterior and causes a man who carries his own "cold within him" to physically sweat (*ibid.*). Scrooge doubts his senses and his sanity and in doing so starts to erode his formally concrete ego. The Ghost of Christmas Past connects and reconciles Scrooge with a former self (meaning that Scrooge can experience empathy, while not quite moving outside of egotism) while The Ghost of Christmas Present turns this newly discovered capacity outwards to encompass the people whom Scrooge's current behaviour effects. By the final vision, Scrooge's concept of self has been obfuscated to such an extent that he fails to recognise what is obvious to the reader; that the unseen "dead man" (p. 100) is him. His sense of community, conversely, has grown to such an extent that he starts to define his own worth not in personal terms but in social terms (he asks to see examples of other people negatively affected by his death). This nuanced psychological shift and progressively outward-looking social stance makes the visions difficult to endure and it is this transformative process which redeems Scrooge as much as the suffering which is its byproduct.

In conclusion then, throughout *A Christmas Carol* redemption functions on two levels: a traditional Christian level in accordance with well-established patterns of redemptive suffering, and a distinctly modern socio-psychological level in which Scrooge is redeemed not just in a moral sense but in a social (or secularly moral) sense by reconfiguring the relationship between self and community. Ultimately, however, the two go hand in hand, with redemptive suffering occurring as a product of personal and social revelations. It is worth noting that this interplay between the religious and the secular can been seen throughout *A Christmas Carol*, not least in its presentation of the concept of Christmas itself.

ISOLATION

The theme of isolation looms large throughout *A Christmas Carol*. Dickens presents us with several instances of isolation and, in almost every case, his characters strive to reverse their situation, or at least establish some form of human contact. The workers at the "solitary" lighthouse find companionship, joining "their horny hands over the rough table" (p. 86) and the Cornish mining families, geographically isolated on a "bleak and desert moor" (p. 85) still gather together for Christmas "decked out gaily in their holiday attire" (*ibid.*). The sole exception, of course, is Scrooge himself, who is characterised by a relentless and completely self-enforced isolation. From his first appearance he is "secret and self-contained, and solitary as an oyster" (p. 34), a man who repeatedly requests to be "left alone" (p. 39) and whose desire for isolation is so strong and so patently apparent that children and animals seem to know it on an instinctual level and avoid him accordingly. He is also geographically isolated to an extent, both alone in his counting house when we are first introduced to him, and living in a "forgotten" and out of the way building with no other tenants (p. 41).

Given that Dickens makes it clear that Scrooge has cultivated his own isolation and that "warning all human sympathy to keep its distance [...] was the very thing he liked" (pp. 34-35), it is particularly interesting to note his emotional reaction to his own, presumable externally enforced, childhood isolation. When the Ghost of Christmas Past presents Scrooge with a vision of his young self, a "lonely boy" in a "long, bare, melancholy room" (p. 58), the sole boarder remaining at school over the Christmas break, Scrooge immediately sits down and weeps, an implicit admission of the fact that social isolation is pitiable, and very probably not a "thing he like[s]" (p. 34). There is a second interesting aspect to this scene which is that while we see young Scrooge "intent upon his reading" (p. 58) (an introverted, self-contained activity), we also simultaneously see the characters he is reading about projected around the classroom, and interacting with him, suggesting that what appears at first to be a method of self-isolation is actually an muddled attempt at 'human' interaction. The larger implication is perhaps that the adult Scrooge's deliberate isolation is a defensive, protective position in response to this early loneliness.

It is also useful to consider isolation as a method of tracking Scrooge's redemption. In many ways his transformation is characterised not just by a newfound generosity but by a newfound sociability: by the end of the final vision he actively wants to rejoin, and become an active part of, his community, to reverse his self-imposed isolation. His central revelation is not just that he has harmed other people but that, as Fred points out, the real result of his misanthropy is that he himself suffers, that "the consequence of his not making merry is that he loses some pleasant moments" (p. 88).

Equally, and finally, there is a compelling case to be made for the idea of Scrooge as isolated, not only from the society around him, but ultimately from himself, or rather his true, original self. The ease with which he cries upon arriving in the past, even before seeing Young Scrooge, suggests an emotional and psychological struggle, and he simultaneously remembers and represses details of his early life (he claims to know the way to the schoolhouse by heart, though the spirit observes he has "forgotten it all these years", p. 57). It is clear to the reader that Scrooge has distanced himself from the version of him which dances, excited, through Fezziwig's ball, but it is this "former, and not latter self" (p. 64) whom he reconnects with, post-redemption, when he laughs and "frisk[s]" through his deserted lodgings (p. 111). With this reading in mind, the whole narrative of *A Christmas Carol* becomes a journey of reconciliation with the self, of Scrooge coming to terms with his own humanity, after which he can fully embrace society and his community more generally.

A CHRISTMAS CAROL AND THE INVENTION OF CHRISTMAS

Since its first publication in 1843, *A Christmas Carol* has not once been out of print, and it has grown into a perennial Christmas favourite, with readings and performances of it as much a part of the Western Christmas tradition as mistletoe and turkey. It is also what Paul Davies refers to as a culture-text: a story so well known, so embedded in the collective consciousness that it can be modified and played with to express modern concerns or themes. In short, it has influenced and continues to influence the concept of Christmas itself in the public imagination.

This was also true at the time of its publication, and in fact there is a case to be made for Dickens inventing (or at least reinventing) Christmas entirely through his writing. His association with the festive period was well established and he published yearly 'Christmas writings' in various London periodicals (of which *A Christmas Carol* is the most famous example, but which also included lesser known titles such as *A Christmas Tree* [1850] and *What Christmas is as We Grow Older* [1851]) and he was, in the public imagination, almost synonymous with Christmas itself. Dickens' biographer Theodore Watts-Dunton records an East End barrow-girl asking, upon hearing of the authors' death, "Dickens dead? Then will Father Christmas die too?" (p. xi). This popular conflation can be attributed at least in part to the fact that, early in his career, and in *A Christmas Carol* especially, Dickens tapped into and helped to shape an already blossoming festive revival.

Throughout the 1820s and 1830s there was a strong interest amongst the upper echelons of society in rediscovering a Christmas of 'the good old days'; a poetic ideal inspired by images of medieval Christmas banquets and based less on Christian worship and piety (which had been the defining tone of Christmas for the previous century or so) and more on merry hearth-side excess and broad principles of good will. This trend gathered speed and spread to the general populace in the 1840s, fed by nostalgia for a (possibly fictional) period when cheer and food were more plentiful (the 'Hungry Forties' was a decade of economic downturn and civil unrest). Generally speaking, by the time Dickens published *A Christmas Carol* a national Christmas revival was already underway, which, while it was still deeply Christian, placed a firm emphasis on merriment rather than on solemnity.

In some respects, then, *A Christmas Carol* was a product of its time. It too hovers between presentations of a traditional Christian Christmas (see Tiny Tim and Bob Cratchit's piety) and a new, more secular and joyful Christmas (see Fezziwig's annual ball). But it also introduces a set of moral values which, however much we may associate them with Christmas now, were not a fully-established part of either Christmas tradition (though they were a very well-established part of Dickens' literary back-catalogue): the idea of a Christmas social conscience, and of generosity of spirit specifically towards the poor and destitute. Even if we accept that Dickens did not entirely invent these, he certainly cemented them in relation to Christmas, as well as emphasising the idea of Christmas as a time to cherish community (whether in the sense of a smaller family unit, or a larger social group). Dickens himself acknowledged his role, and the role of the novella, in establishing these festive principles, terming this emphasis on generosity of spirit towards your fellow man *his* 'Carol Philosophy'.

In conclusion, then, while *A Christmas Carol* was shaped by the pre-existing mid-Victorian Christmas revival, it was also instrumental in shaping it in turn, and part of the reason why the novella feels so inherently festive to a modern audience is because it helped to establish many of the themes and images that we now associate with Christmas itself.

FURTHER REFLECTION

SOME QUESTIONS TO THINK ABOUT...

- Discuss food and the role of food in *A Christmas Carol*. What sorts of food does Dickens describe and what does food represent more generally?
- "You fear the world too much," she answered, gently. "All your other hopes have merged into the hope of being beyond the chance of its sordid reproach" (p. 65). Discuss the role of fear in *A Christmas Carol* with reference both to its supernatural elements and other, more terrestrial, sources of fear.
- Compare and contrast the characters of Fan (Scrooge's sister) and Tiny Tim. What physical and personal traits do they share? What is the effect of this on Scrooge's redemptive journey?
- "A lonely boy was reading near a feeble fire; and Scrooge sat down upon a form, and wept to see his poor forgotten self as he used to be" (p. 58). Reread the passage in Stave Two detailing Scrooge's school years (p. 56-61). To what

extent do you believe that Scrooge's childhood explains his adult behaviour? Does it excuse it as well?

- A key theme of *A Christmas Carol* is the triumph of emotional vulnerability over Victorian ideals of masculinity. Discuss.

- Discuss the presentation of family (and family-like social groups) in the novella. Can Dickens' vision of an ideal Christmas exist independently from his vision of the ideal Victorian family?

- Consider Dickens' authorial voice, and his sometimes meaningful, often humorous asides to the audience throughout *A Christmas Carol*. What is the larger function of this device?

- Consider the role of time and how time itself functions in *A Christmas Carol*. How do the Christmas ghosts distort time and to what effect?

- Compare and contrast *A Christmas Carol* with one or more of its film adaptations. Have any parts of Dickens' original text been omitted? Why do you think this is? Do the film adaptations reflect the period/country in which they were made as much as they do Dickensian London?

We want to hear from you!
Leave a comment on your online library
and share your favourite books on social media!

FURTHER READING

REFERENCE EDITION

- Dickens, C. (2003) *A Christmas Carol and Other Christmas Writings*. London: Penguin

REFERENCE STUDIES

- Davies, P. (1990) The Lives and Times of Ebenezer Scrooge. New Haven: Yale University Press.

ADAPTATIONS

- *Scrooge.* (1951) [Film]. Brian Desmond Hurst. Dir. UK/USA: Renown Pictures.
- *A Christmas Carol.* (1999) [Television film]. David Jones. Dir. UK/USA: RHI Entertainment.
- *A Christmas Carol.* (2009) [Film]. Robert Zemekis. Dir. USA: Walt Disney Pictures.

MORE FROM BRIGHTSUMMARIES.COM

- Reading guide – Bleak House by Charles Dickens.
- Reading guide – David Copperfield by Charles Dickens.

- Reading guide – Great Expectations by Charles Dickens.

- Reading guide – Hard Times by Charles Dickens.

- Reading guide – Oliver Twist by Charles Dickens.

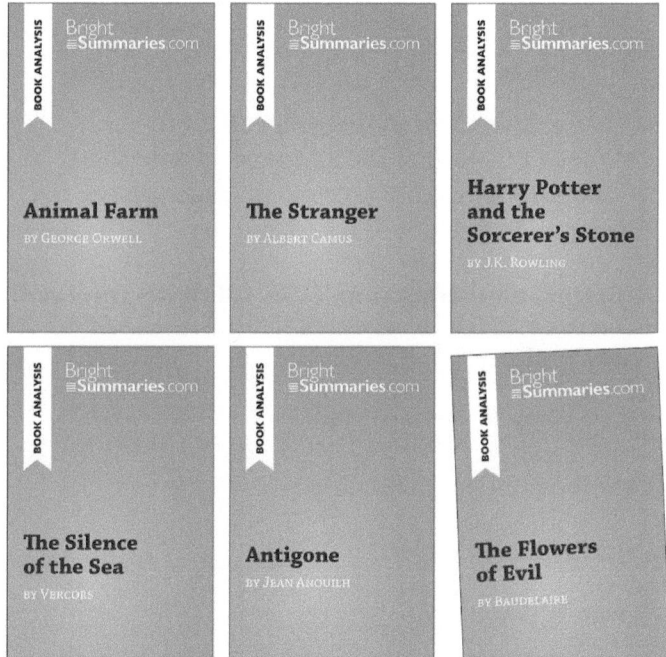

www.brightsummaries.com

Ebook EAN: 9782808018340

Paperback EAN: 9782808018357

Legal Deposit: D/2019/12603/84

Cover: © Primento

Digital conception by Primento, the digital partner of publishers.